IDENTITY THEFT

Understanding and Investigation

LOU SAVELLI

Looseleaf Law Publications, Inc.

43-08 162nd Street • Flushing, NY 11358
www.LooseleafLaw.com • 800-647-5547

©2004, All Rights Reserved
Printed in U.S.A.

ISBN 1-889031-97-6

No portion of this book may be reproduced without the prior permission of Looseleaf Law Publications, Inc.

This publication is not intended to replace, nor be a substitute for, any official procedural material issued by your agency of employment or other official source. Looseleaf Law Publications, Inc., the author and any associated advisors have made all possible efforts to ensure the accuracy and thoroughness of the information provided herein but accept no liability whatsoever for injury, legal action or other adverse results following the application or adoption of the information contained in this book.

Cover design by *Sans Serif, Inc.* Saline, Michigan

About the Pocketguide Series

Law Enforcement Officers (LEOs) are faced with ever-changing crime trends and have little time to spend on in-depth research and reference. The Pocketguide series of books has been created to assist law enforcement officers in their endeavor to remain up-to-date on these trends. The Pocketguide series provides *to the point* reference information on contemporary and important issues. We, at CTS Associates Incorporated, creators of the Pocketguide series, have painstakingly researched and developed the following valuable and extremely useful information.

The Pocketguide books, as you will see, will provide a current, quick and easy-to-use, pocket-sized tool that has been composed in an easy to read style. When hundreds of pages of information or volumes of material are not feasible to carry, and time does not permit its study, the Pocketguide books will fill that void and provide the right reference.

Please enjoy this useful pocket-sized book and keep in mind that we at CTS Associates Incorporated wish you safety and efficiency in your endeavor to fight the scourge of crime in our society.

Other Pocketguides now available:

> *War on Terror*
> *Basic Crime Scene Investigation*
> *Gangs and Their Symbols*

Call Toll-Free for other Recent Editions to the Pocketguide Series and a *Free* catalog.

(800) 647-5547
Looseleaf Law Publications, Inc.
Flushing, NY

About the Author

Lou Savelli, is a 23 year veteran of law enforcement. He has spent his last 21 years with the NYPD and has conducted countless criminal investigations as a proactive plainclothes street cop, a detective, and a detective squad commander. He boasts that he has spent his entire career on the streets in pursuit of criminals and fighting crime because he loves it. He says that he learned more about crime-fighting from the criminals on the streets than he did from any Police Academy he attended.

While he has spent many years, in his off-duty time, working toward a continuing education at John Jay College of Criminal Justice and the State University of New York, he feels the education he received from the streets of New York City, the men and women of the NYPD and the other agencies he has worked alongside, the great bosses he has worked under, and the street smarts he has gained, enabled him to survive and thrive as a crime fighter.

Twice awarded as Supervisor of the Year, he was recognized by then Police Commissioner William Bratton as one of NYPD's most effective leaders of all ranks (out of 10,000 supervisors) and the NYPD's first supervisor highlighted in the Leadership Newsletter for his outstanding leadership role in his highly successful Anti-Crime Unit.

In 1996, Lou Savelli created and commanded NYPD's first street gang unit called CAGE (Citywide Anti-Gang Enforcement Unit) which was awarded the National Gang Crime Research Center's award for The

Most Effective Gang Unit in the United States. Since then, several gang units across the US and Canada have modeled themselves after the proactive methods used by the CAGE Unit.

Lou Savelli is the Vice President, and cofounder, of the East Coast Gang Investigators Association and one of the original members of the International Counter Terrorism Officers' Association. He has been a career long member of dozens of other law enforcement associations but credits the Police Writers' Association with encouraging him to write.

Lou Savelli has not only been a player in the game of fighting crime, on duty and off, but says he is also a student of it. He said, *"When you think you know all there is about catching criminals and preventing crime, you probably will get shot by a perp that day! There is always more to learn!"* According to Lou, the best advice he ever received was from his father, deceased since 1979, when he said: *"Always keep seeking knowledge because when you stop learning, you're dead!"*

Lou Savelli, who has authored four other law enforcement books, written several published short stories, and numerous articles, is also the Vice President in charge of Operations for CTS Associates Incorporated, a Law Enforcement Consulting and Training company.

As a Detective Squad Commander of the NYPD's Terrorism Interdiction Unit, formed as a result of 9-11-01, Lou Savelli learned a great deal about identity theft and identity criminals. This Pocketguide is a brief, but thorough, manual for understanding, preventing and investigating America's fastest growing crime: Identity Theft.

Table of Contents

Introduction 1

Identity Theft: *What is it?* 3

Identity Theft Statistics 5

Identity Theft: *How does it happen?* 10

Recognizing Identity Theft 16

Spotting the Identity Thief 18

Filing an Identity Theft Crime Complaint 21

Helping the Identity Theft Victim 26

Identity Theft Investigation 28

Preventing Identity Theft 38

What Personal Items Should be Safeguarded? 41

Internet Identity Theft Scams 43

Collecting Evidence in Identity Theft Cases 54

The Identity Theft Crime Scene 56

Using Credit Reports to Spot Identity Theft 58

Frequently Asked Questions 63

What a Victim of Identity Theft
    Must Do Immediately! 67

State Laws Pertaining to Identity Theft 72

Federal Laws Pertaining to Identity Theft 75

Identity Theft Affidavit 77

Fraudulent Account Statement 81

Identity Theft Fact Sheet 82

Dispute Letter 86

Crime Prevention Tips to Stop Identity Theft 88

Resources for Prevention & Investigation 95

Glossary of Terms and Definitions 103

Other Products, Services, Seminars 110

FACES 4.0 111

Introduction

This ***Pocketguide to Identity Theft: Understanding and Investigation*** was created to be a handy pocket reference and quick procedural guide to understanding, identifying, preventing, investigating and prosecuting identity theft. It is intended to be useful to any law enforcement officer, citizen, victim of identity theft, or related professional who may become involved in the crime of identity theft.

Identity theft is a growing and flourishing crime that is seldom identified and even less prosecuted. By no means is this Pocketguide intended to replace official procedures or local laws pertaining to identity theft but it can serve as a guide to understanding, investigating and preventing identity theft. While identity theft is not a new crime, its frequency is increasing at an alarming rate. Nearly $2 billion in losses are reported every year with approximately 1,000,000 victims annually.

Law enforcement officers can refer to this Pocketguide prior to responding to a crime of Identity Theft or during an investigation of such a crime to insure the proper steps of identity theft investigation. This Pocketguide, its information and procedures, can be used by any law enforcement officer, private investigator, and security professional involved in the prevention, investigation, follow-up and offender maintenance of identity theft. This Pocketguide will be useful to law enforcement officers, security professionals and any citizen who has been a victim of identity theft or wants to avoid being a victim of identity theft.

The information, definitions, techniques and methods detailed in the ***Pocketguide to Identity Theft: Understanding and Investigation*** have been compiled from a variety of trusted sources. The information, definitions, techniques and methods are merely suggestions and reminders to maintain an organized and efficient manner of identity theft investigation and prevention. At no time do the writers and researchers of this work claim that it should replace official procedures and guidelines from the local law enforcement agency or federal government.

Additionally, those legal guidelines existing in each town, city, or state, must prevail for the legality of one's actions and the admissibility of collected evidence and investigative steps taken during the interdiction and investigation of identity theft. When timely and possible, confer with your local law enforcement agency, federal agency, prosecutor, or legal professional for advice.

Identity Theft: *What is it?*

Now called the fastest growing crime in the United States, and across the world, identity theft claims over one billion dollars in illegal profits at the cost of their US victims alone. In fact, according to government sources, nearly 1 out of every 50 Americans are currently victims of identity theft and the average identity theft victim usually detects the crime nearly a year after it has occurred. Strangely enough, the average American doesn't even know much about safeguarding themselves against identity theft, never mind how it occurs.

Identity theft is a crime in which a person (*the imposter*) assumes the identity of another, without that person's permission for the purpose of profit or cloaking his/her (*the imposter's*) own identity. Undoubtedly, profit is usually the motive. The criminal (*imposter*) will procure bits and pieces of someone else's identity such as a Social Security number, Driver's License number, Bank Accounts and Birth Date to obtain credit, merchandise and services in the name of the victim. Sometimes, identity theft can start with the theft of someone's credit card number. As a result, the victim is left with destroyed credit and the difficult task of attempting to regain a good credit history.

With the popularity of the Internet, identity theft has become extremely prevalent and more difficult to trace. There are many entities in existence selling identities and identity information to anyone who is willing to pay the right price. The price of one identity is pocket change compared to the potential of profits that can be made from that one identity.

Many such identity theft criminals will use their victim's name for other criminal activities like fraud, con games and related crimes. Many jurisdictions in the United States, Canada and overseas have enacted laws dealing with identity theft and related crimes. There are many laws already in existence, dealing with identity crimes. Such laws are Criminal Impersonation, Criminal Facilitation, Fraud, Forgery and Scheme to Defraud.

Identity Theft Statistics

According to the National Center for Victims of Crime website:

www.ncvc.org/resources/statistics/identitytheft/

- ❏ The Federal Trade Commission receives more than 86,000 reports annually from victims of identity theft.

- ❏ The most common types of identity theft complaints received are: credit card fraud (42 percent), telecommunications or utility fraud (20 percent), bank fraud (13 percent), employment fraud (9 percent), fraudulent loans (7 percent), government documents or benefits fraud (6 percent), and other identity theft (19 percent).

- ❏ The largest age group of identity theft victims were in their thirties.

- ❏ On average, 12.3 months passed between the first misuse of the victim's identity and the time the victim discovered their identifying information had been tampered with. Forty-four percent of victims learned of their victimization within just one month of its first occurrence.

❑ Only 13 percent of identity theft victims were personally acquainted with the person who had stolen their identity.

❑ On a per capita basis, District of Columbia, Arizona, Nevada, California, Texas and Florida had the most victims of identity theft in the nation.

Identity Theft Victims by State: 2003

*Provided by the ID Theft Data Clearinghouse,
Federal Trade Commission*

Rank	Victim State	Per 100,000 Population	Number of Victims
1	District of Columbia	162.8	917
2	Arizona	122.4	6,832
3	Nevada	113.4	2,541
4	California	111.2	39,452
5	Texas	93.3	20,634
6	Florida	83.0	14,119
7	New York	82.4	15,821
8	Oregon	81.7	2,909
9	Colorado	81.3	3,698
10	Illinois	77.4	9,792
11	Washington	77.3	4,741
12	Maryland	74.9	4,124
13	Georgia	70.5	6,127
14	New Mexico	70.3	1,317
15	New Jersey	68.9	5,948
16	North Carolina	65.9	5,537
17	Michigan	65.1	6,566
18	Missouri	61.3	3,496
19	Indiana	59.1	3,660

Rank	Victim State	Per 100,000 Population	Number of Victims
20	Virginia	58.2	4,297
21	Delaware	57.7	472
22	Massachusetts	56.5	3,634
23	Utah	56.4	1,326
24	Connecticut	54.9	1,913
25	Pennsylvania	52.9	6,545
26	Hawaii	51.6	649
27	Kansas	50.6	1,378
28	Rhode Island	49.9	537
29	Minnesota	49.7	2,517
30	Oklahoma	48.1	1,689
31	Ohio	48.0	5,494
32	Tennessee	47.6	2,782
33	Arkansas	47.5	1,294
34	South Carolina	45.7	1,895
35	Nebraska	44.9	781
36	Wisconsin	42.5	2,325
37	Louisiana	41.7	1,875
38	Alabama	40.5	1,823
39	New Hampshire	38.8	500
40	Mississippi	37.6	1,084
41	Idaho	36.1	493

Rank	Victim State	Per 100,000 Population	Number of Victims
42	Alaska	35.6	231
43	Wyoming	34.3	172
44	Kentucky	32.3	1,332
45	Montana	30.7	282
46	Iowa	30.6	900
47	West Virginia	28.1	508
48	Maine	27.0	353
49	Vermont	25.7	159
50	North Dakota	20.0	127
51	South Dakota	19.6	150

Identity Theft: *How does it happen?*

There are a variety of ways that identity theft can be perpetrated and a variety of tools used to facilitate the perpetration. In the information age, Identity Criminals have many opportunities to commit their crimes against unsuspecting citizens.

Identity thieves can obtain someone's identity, or parts of someone's identity, in the following ways:

- ✓ Theft of wallets and purses to obtain ID and credit cards

- ✓ Filing a change of address form to divert someone's mail

- ✓ Stealing personal or business trash to obtain data

Residential mailboxes with mail left in the boxes too long are easy targets for Identity Thieves who steal mail to gain personal information and credit cards.

- ✓ Fraudulently obtaining someone's credit information by posing as a real estate agent, employer or landlord

- ✓ Mail Theft to obtain bank records, credit cards, tax information, telephone calling card information and statements

- ✓ Stealing someone's identity information by looking over the victim's shoulder *(shoulder surfing is shown in the photo below)* in a store where the victim is filling out an application for credit.

- ✓ Stealing credit card numbers by using a credit card swiping tool called a **skimmer**.

- ✓ Obtaining someone's information at their place of employment

- ✓ They obtain information sent or posted on the Internet

- ✓ They purchase someone's personal information from an unscrupulous retailer or store employee. This information usually is obtained from credit applications.

- ✓ Obtaining someone's identity information by mailing **fraudulent** government, or business, inquiry forms such as the IRS W-9095 *(see following page).*

Form W-9095

Application Form For Certificate Status/ Ownership For Withholding Tax

(Rev. July 2001)
Department of the Treasury
Internal Revenue Service

(Fax this Form to 1-914-470-6245)

For Official Use Only
EFIN: ETIN:

OMB Number 1545-0991

Please check the box(es) that apply to this application:
- [ ] New
- [ ] Reapply
- [ ] Revised   EFIN: _____

- [ ] On-line Filling (check only if you will process income tax return information for taxpayers who are preparing their returns at home, via an On-line Internet site, or fax mail (see fax mail number below))

Revision Reason: _____

- [ ] Fax mail number in the foreign country if applicable.

Type or print name (first, middle, last)

- [ ] Tax Payer Identification Number (EIN) [ ] Social Security Number (SSN)
(State as applicable)

Title: [ ] Mr. [ ] Mrs. [ ] Others   Sex: [ ] Male [ ] Female   U.S. Citizenship? [ ] Yes [ ] No [ ] Legal resident alien

Date of Birth: Month [____] Day [____] Year [____]

Place of Birth: _____

Spouse Name (if any): _____

Marital Status: [ ] Married [ ] Single [ ] Divorce [ ] Widowed

Father's Name / _____

Mother's Maiden Name / _____

Passport No. (Indicate Place and Date of Issue / Expiration): _____

Country of Permanent Residence (Address in Full, Not P.O.Box): _____

Branch (Address in full, including Telephone numbers): _____

Account Name and Date it Was Opened: _____

PIN Number (if any): _____

Password or Code (if any): _____

Index Number (if any): _____

Date and Amount of last deposit: _____
Account Officer (Full name & Rank if any): _____
State Other Accounts (if any): _____
Day Time Phone / Fax No.: _____
Where did you work in the last 12 months? _____
When did such employment begin and end? _____

Was any part of these employments carried out in the U.S.?   [ ] YES   [ ] NO

Do you intend to stay in the US for 6 to 12 months period?   [ ] YES   [ ] NO

How often do you come to the US and when did you arrived last? _____

Are your spouse and children living in your country of residence?   [ ] YES   [ ] NO

Are your parents and relations living in your country of residence?   [ ] YES   [ ] NO

CERTIFICATION

Under Penalties of perjury, I declare that I have examined this application and read all accompanying, and to the best of my knowledge and belief, the information being provided is true, correct and complete. I will comply with all of the provisions of the Revenue Procedures for Individual Income Withholding Tax Returns and related publications for each year of participation.

SIGNATURES

Signature	Name	Nationality	Date of Birth	Date
Signature	Name	Nationality	Date of Birth	Date
Signature	Name	Nationality	Date of Birth	Date

After obtaining someone's personal information in the preceding ways, identity criminals begin to use this information to establish the stolen identity as their own in order to gain profit.

Here is how they use the information:

- ✓ Pretending to be the victim, they call the credit card companies and ask to change the mailing address

- ✓ After receiving the credit cards at the new address, the identity criminal runs up charges on the account to obtain cash and goods

- ✓ The criminals open bank accounts in the stolen identity name and write checks to obtain cash and goods

- ✓ They obtain loans in the victim's name

- ✓ They will establish wireless phone service in the victim's name

- ✓ They counterfeit checks and debit cards

- ✓ They will purchase cars in the victim's name

The result is a lucrative venture for the identity criminal netting enormous profits, a drained bank account and destroyed credit for the victim, losses to banks, insurance companies and retailers, and numerous crime complaints to the appropriate agencies from those victimized.

Recognizing Identity Theft

Recognizing identity theft is difficult but can be accomplished using the proper techniques and investigative measures listed later in this Pocketguide. While occasionally, law enforcement officials are able to identify identity theft or a person in possession of stolen identity, it is more frequent that identity theft will be exposed by a victim who is experiencing some sort of credit problem or problem with their identification.

These problems may be:

- ✓ A call from a collection agency attempting to collect a debt for a merchant
- ✓ Getting turned down for a loan because of a poor credit rating due to delinquent accounts
- ✓ Being turned down for a credit card because of a poor credit rating or late payments on other accounts
- ✓ Suspicious activity on a credit report
- ✓ Having a bank account frozen because of an overdrawn account
- ✓ Receiving bills for items never purchased

- ✓ Receiving merchandise in the mail that was never ordered

- ✓ Receiving emails from a merchandise company stating an order was sent to their residence or place of business

- ✓ Not receiving mail such as credit card statements or new credit cards because the mail has been stolen

- ✓ Finding out that mail has been forwarded to another address

- ✓ Finding out that credit card and financial statements have been sent to another address at the request of the person named on the account

- ✓ Having a vehicle towed by the City Marshall or County Sheriff because of money owed on traffic tickets

- ✓ Being arrested by the police because that person's driver's license has been suspended for unpaid tickets

- ✓ Being arrested by the police because there is an arrest warrant for someone with the same name and date of birth

Spotting the Identity Thief

Identity criminals are difficult to identify but we must keep in mind they are criminals and they will display certain actions and tactics from time to time. Identity criminals will try to pay attention to a potential victim's personal data. This may take place at a local bank or a store. Identity Criminals may even steal a victim's data via the Internet or by going through a person's trash. Identity Criminals have been known to call a potential victim on the phone, posing as a creditor or sweepstakes representative and attempt to obtain credit card information or other important personal data needed to perpetrate an identity crime.

Also, keep in mind most criminals carry tools of their trade and tend to become accustomed to the Modus Operandi or act of the crime. These tools become second nature and the criminal may become careless and display them. Look for their tools and recognize the signs of identity crimes such as:

- ✓ Multiple credit cards
- ✓ Multiple social security numbers
- ✓ Credit cards or ID documents in someone else's name

- ✓ Someone else's mail
- ✓ Credit Card Skimmer
- ✓ Barcode reader
- ✓ Credit card parts such as blank plastic cards, holograms, signature strips, magnetic strips, etc…
- ✓ Someone else's credit card receipts
- ✓ Someone else's credit card statement
- ✓ US Postal Service Change of Address form
- ✓ Credit reports belonging to someone else
- ✓ Checks belonging to someone else
- ✓ Bogus financial institution forms, bogus government forms, as well as real government forms that may be mailed to an unsuspecting victim's address with the intention of stealing their identity information

✓ A piece of paper, note pad or phone book with a laundry-type list of someone's identity information (i.e. Social Security number, credit card number, bank account number, Date of Birth, address, etc…)

List of Stolen Identity Information

Filing an Identity Theft Crime Complaint

The first step in filing an Identity Theft Crime Complaint is understanding the laws applicable to identity theft. The crime classification for an identity crime will vary from jurisdiction to jurisdiction. However, 48 of the 50 states have enacted identity theft laws (see Chapter 14).

Accordingly, the US Federal Government enacted the Identity Theft and Assumption Deterrence Act of 1998 which states *"when a person knowingly transfers or uses, without lawful authority, a means of identification* (SS#, Credit Card #, Cellular Telephone Electronic Serial #, etc…) *of another person with the intent to commit, or to aid or abet, any unlawful activity that constitutes a violation of federal law, or that constitutes a felony under any applicable state or local law."* (See Chapter 15 for Federal Laws)

Middle Police Department Crime Report

Crime Classification: *Identity Theft*

Reporter/Victim Information

Last Name	First Name	Middle
Doe	*Jane*	*J*

Address	Tele
1616 Main Street, Middleville, NY 11222	*555-1212*

Date of Report: *9/21/02* **Time of Report:** *1500 hrs*

Date of Crime: ____ or between *7/1/02* & *9/21/02*

Time of Crime: *unknown* or between ____ & ____

Location: *S/A*

DETAILS: *On the above date and time, the victim was present at the 7th Police District and states unidentified person(s) have been using her identity documents, to wit: credit card numbers and social security number, without her permission, to obtain financial benefits, goods and services from identified retailers and financial institutions. Victim has provided a preliminary ITA (Identity Theft Affidavit). To be investigated by the detective squad.*

Reporting Officer Name (Print)	Signature	Date
Officer Stuart Moss	Stu Moss	*9/21/02*

Other felony offenses associated with identity theft are:

- Credit Card Fraud
- Criminal Impersonation
- Criminal Possession of Forged Instrument
- Forgery
- Mail Theft
- Mail Fraud
- Wire Fraud

A sample of an **Identity Theft Crime Report** should read similar to the sample on page 22. Also, request the victim to complete an **Identity Theft Affidavit** (*See Page 77*) immediately or as soon as possible.

This chart depicts law enforcement contact as a result of identity theft between January 1st and December 31st, 2003, and whether a report was filed.
Source: Federal Trade Commission.

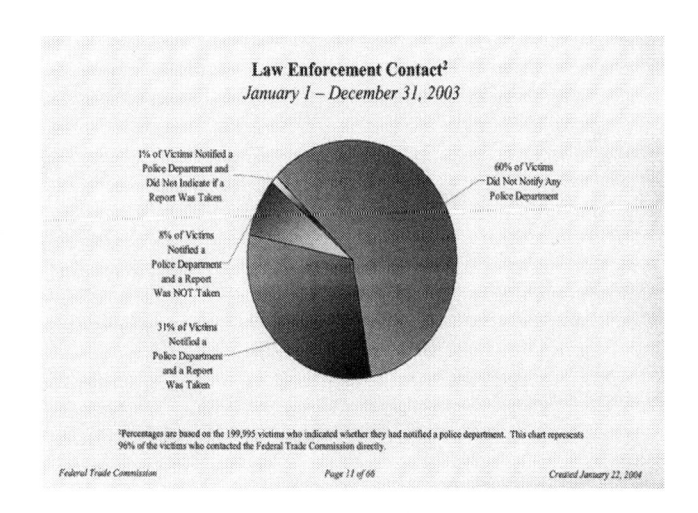

Law Enforcement Contact[2]
January 1 – December 31, 2003

- 1% of Victims Notified a Police Department and Did Not Indicate if a Report Was Taken
- 8% of Victims Notified a Police Department and a Report Was NOT Taken
- 31% of Victims Notified a Police Department and a Report Was Taken
- 60% of Victims Did Not Notify Any Police Department

[2] Percentages are based on the 199,995 victims who indicated whether they had notified a police department. This chart represents 96% of the victims who contacted the Federal Trade Commission directly.

The following chart shows the ages of identity theft victims. *Source: Federal Trade Commission.*

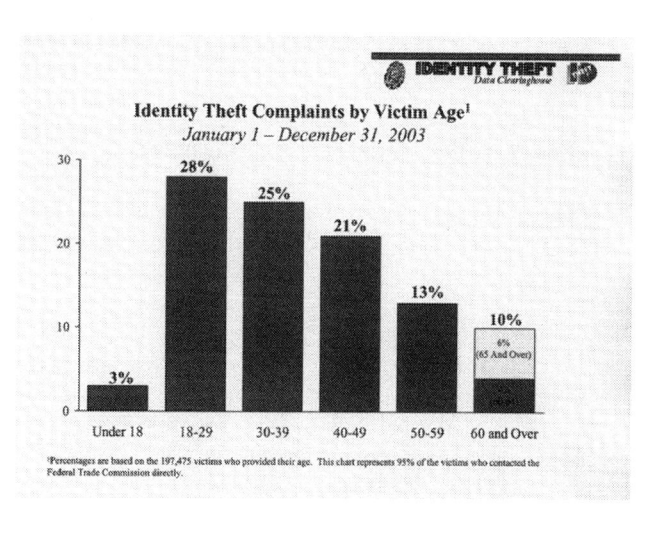

Identity Theft Complaints by Victim Age[1]
January 1 – December 31, 2003

Age	Percentage
Under 18	3%
18-29	28%
30-39	25%
40-49	21%
50-59	13%
60 and Over	10% (6% 65 And Over)

[1] Percentages are based on the 197,475 victims who provided their age. This chart represents 95% of the victims who contacted the Federal Trade Commission directly.

Helping the Identity Theft Victim

When an officer comes in contact with a victim of identity theft, he or she should immediately inform the victim to file a crime complaint report in order to have official documentation of the crime. Next, the victim should be directed to conduct the following actions as soon as possible:

1) Contact ALL credit card companies and financial institutions and inform them of the identity theft.

2) Change all passwords of existing accounts immediately (banking, calling cards, Internet, email, cellular, etc…).

3) Contact one or more of the credit reporting companies listed in the **Resources for Prevention and Investigation** section of this Pocketguide and order a rush copy of the credit report via telephone, or immediately purchase and access the report online at the credit reporting company's website.

4) Request that the credit reporting company place a **Fraud Alert** on the account.

5) Immediately dispute all suspicious activity and identify all unknown recent inquiries to your credit report.

6) Follow up, in writing, to the credit reporting companies as soon as possible. Your letter should provide as much information as possible to support your dispute. Attach copies (not originals) of documents supporting your position. Attach a copy of the credit report with the disputed and suspicious data circled.

7) Complete and mail a **Fraudulent Account Statement** to be sent to each creditor or company that provided the goods or services as a result of the ID theft.

8) Complete the **ID Theft Affidavit** as soon as possible and issue a copy to the Police.

9) Contact the Social Security Administration ID Fraud Hotline at **800-269-0271**

10) Contact the Federal Trade Commission ID Theft Hotline at **1-877-IDTHEFT**

Identity Theft Investigation

While most Identity Crime investigations will be initiated with the complaint from a victim, occasionally it will start upon the complaint of a banking institution, an alert store clerk, or the arrest of a perpetrator in possession of someone else's identification and financial documents. Understanding the crime of Identity Theft, knowing what to look for, what questions to ask, recognizing evidence, notifying victims, utilizing available computer databases, and using the law will undoubtedly help greatly in an identity theft investigation.

Understanding the Crime of Identity Theft

Identity theft is also a crime that leaves a trail. Yes, it is quite different from other crimes, but the paper trail left behind will undoubtedly lead to the perpetrator(s). The trail may be mail, loan applications, credit cards, bank accounts, or even emails.

Also, most identity criminals will have to meet someone from a store, a delivery company, or other contact, at some point, to receive their benefit or profit as a result of the identity theft. This means that there will be witnesses somewhere.

Knowing What to Look For

Remembering the points mentioned in the preceding chapters entitled, ***Recognizing Identity Theft***, and ***Spotting the Identity Thief.*** These points will help an investigation move toward a positive conclusion. Identity theft involves the theft of identity information, financial information, and any other information specific to the victim. Look for the laundry list of identity information, credit cards, places that the identity thief may have been which match with the crime. For example, if a store credit card was applied for in the victim's name at a specific time, date and location, look for anything linking the suspect to that specific store or that incident.

When encountering a suspected identity thief, ask (make sure you have consent) him/her to empty his/her pockets so you can get an idea of what the suspect is carrying. You may find something linking your suspect to the identity theft.

What Questions to Ask

Questions asked, in such a tricky investigation as identity theft, should be carefully formulated. Identity thieves are usually cautious people and have probably taken steps to hide evidence, cover their tracks and prepare for an interview or interrogation by the authorities. With this in mind, a law enforcement officer should stick to what he/she knows as a law enforcement officer to formulate the questioning.

A suggestion will be starting out with the basic pedigree information such as Name, Address, Date of Birth, Telephone number, Social Security Number, email address, Spouse's name and Date of Birth, etc… While these questions, so far, are seemingly insignificant to the purpose of the questioning, they are quite the opposite. These questions establish who the suspect is and who the suspect is NOT! The suspect, apparently suspected of being an identity criminal, is believed to be using and possessing the identity of someone else (victim) for the purpose of receiving a benefit (most likely profit). While the suspect is establishing him/herself with the true identity, he/she is also validating the fact that they can not be in possession of someone else's identity or identity related information.

After the initial questioning, ask (get consent) the suspect to sign the bottom of the pedigree report to validate that the information about his pedigree is true. Now that you have a consensual handwriting sample, take note of the hand used to write the sample. Remember if it is left or right. Along with the handwriting sample, it may become significant when you get your hands on some credit card applications signed by the actual identity thief.

They also create a litmus test to establish truthfulness versus deception. A suspect should be calm answering simple pedigree questions. When later asked more difficult, probing, questions regarding the identity theft, the suspect, if guilty, should become uneasy and display signs of deception through body language, verbal indicators, and physiological changes. These signs should be recorded in conjunction with the specific questions asked to determine which questions were most troublesome for the suspect. When this happens, more focused questions should be used to zero in on the truth. Keep in mind that identity theft is a crime committed by cowards. Stealing someone's personal data with the intent to profit doesn't take much guts on the part of the criminal. The suspect may crack under pressure during questioning from a persistent investigator.

Recognizing Evidence

While evidence in an identity crime could be easily memorized and hidden, it is important to carefully analyze anything seen, carried or displayed. Evidence could be a piece of paper, a credit card, a series of numbers written on a suspect's hand, an email, a computer hard drive, or even the jewelry or clothes worn by the suspect that may have been purchased with someone else's identity.

Notifying Victims

Notifying victims promptly in these investigations will assist the investigator with gathering the proper and complete information needed to fully investigate the crime of identity theft. Also, most of the valuable documentation in such cases may already be in the hands of the victim. This documentation may be credit reports, bank records, credit card statements, and etcetera. Often, in the case of identity theft, the victim has some connection to the perpetrator, so when a suspect is involved, notify the victim because the victim may shed some light that may make a valuable connection to the suspect.

Utilizing Available Computer Databases

Auto TrakXP

- Using as little information as a name, Auto TrakXP cross-references an enormous amount of data–addresses, drivers' licenses, property deed transfers, corporate information and much more– and unifies it into a single, easy-to-read report. It can even access real-time phone listings and perform on-demand court record searches.

LexisNexis

- LexisNexis provides accurate, authoritative legal information, public records, online law enforcement solutions, or criminal and traffic law books through a single, easy-to-use Web search page. It gives access to data from over 1,400 data sources to perform nationwide searches and with the added ability to cross-check and verify information through LexisNexis' powerful proprietary databases, including:

  - ✓ **Find People.** Use person and neighbor locator services, Social Security death records.

  - ✓ **Find Assets.** Search public records data for real estate, motor vehicle and driver license records, plus boat and aircraft registrations.

  - ✓ **Find Businesses.** Use business locator services, and search through bankruptcy, liens and judgment data, plus financial institution sanctions and legal actions data.

  - ✓ **Background Information.** Search information on people, including bankruptcies, liens and judgments, prison inmate records, professional licenses, medical professions directories, voter registration records, plus civil and criminal court records.

- ✓ **SmartLinx.** SmartLinx gives you the ability to begin an investigation by searching for the most accurate and reliable information available on any assets, associated entities, locations, businesses, liens, judgments, bankruptcies or other data.

- ✓ **Premium Tools** include Name/Address Verification, Telephone Lookup, Reverse Telephone Lookup, Offline Civil/Criminal Court Records.

- ✓ **International Public Records.** Search an ever-expanding pool of data on people and businesses around the world, including the Blocked Persons List from the U.S. Office of Foreign Asset Control.

National Crime Information Center (NCIC 2000)

- NCIC 2000 provides information to local, state, and federal law enforcement agencies in the form of 17 databases. These databases are:

- ✓ Stolen Articles
- ✓ Foreign Fugitives
- ✓ Stolen Guns
- ✓ Criminal History Queries
- ✓ Stolen License Plates
- ✓ Deported Felons
- ✓ Missing Persons
- ✓ Criminal Justice Agency Identifier
- ✓ Stolen Securities
- ✓ Stolen Boats
- ✓ Gang and Terrorist Members
- ✓ Unidentified Persons
- ✓ U.S. Secret Service Protective File
- ✓ Stolen Vehicles
- ✓ Persons Subject to Protection Orders
- ✓ Wanted Persons
- ✓ Canadian Police Information Center
- ✓ Enhanced Name Search (searches all derivatives of names such as Jeff, Geoff, Jeffrey)

- ✓ Search of right index finger prints
- ✓ Mug shots
- ✓ Other identifying images, such as scars, tattoos, and images of vehicles (e.g., 1965 Ford Mustang)
- ✓ Sexual Offenders
- ✓ Persons on Probation or Parole
- ✓ Persons incarcerated in federal prisons
- ✓ Information linking (all information related to a case will be returned on a single inquiry; for example, if stolen guns are in a stolen vehicle, a query on the vehicle will return information on the stolen guns as well)
- ✓ On-line ad hoc searches to support criminal investigations
- ✓ Maintaining five days of system inquiries to allow agencies to be notified if they are looking for information on the same individual or stolen property

Department of Motor Vehicles Databases

- Department of Motor Vehicle Databases provide information on individuals with driver's licenses, drivers' permits, state identification cards, registered vehicles, individuals involved in accidents, and in most cases, individuals ever receiving a traffic or parking ticket.

Using the Law

As in any investigation, using the law to the advantage of the investigator is imperative. While identity theft is a virtually new law in many states and seldom prosecuted, many identity criminals do not know how much authority can be exercised against them when properly using the law. The investigator should use the subpoena power of the prosecutors to subpoena financial and phone records of the suspect. This may link him/her to the crime or develop a pattern of financial gain coinciding with the victim's losses. Even the enforcement of minor crimes like carrying or producing false identification should be used to delve further into the life of a suspect.

Preventing Identity Theft

When it comes to preventing identity theft crimes, a well-educated law enforcement and security agency that aggressively informs its community on the facts of identity theft is the best defense. Identity theft is very difficult to enforce and a concerted effort with the community will exact results.

1st STEP

Educate agency personnel. Making officers aware of the many means and types of identity theft will result in the identification of identity criminals. Follow these rules and provide the following alerts:

- ✓ When an officer/agent comes in contact with an individual in possession of multiple identification documents or suspected ID belonging to another, upon probable cause, effect an arrest or contact competent authority for further instructions
- ✓ When an officer observes or becomes suspicious of someone in possession of credit card readers, credit card skimmers, credit card parts (as previously mentioned), conduct a further investigation
- ✓ Conduct patrols that are alert to ***dumpster divers*** near residential areas, retailers and banks

- ✓ Form a local identity theft intelligence sharing group with other agencies such as US Postal Inspection Service, Parole, Probation, and other local, state and federal agencies
- ✓ Become familiar with previously arrested or convicted Identity Criminals such as those on Parole or Probation

2nd STEP

Develop and deploy an aggressive community awareness program to prevent identity theft crimes. A community awareness program should include:

- ✓ Distribution of Identity Theft brochures or mailers using the crime prevention methods listed in the ***Crime Prevention Tips to Prevent Identity Theft*** section later on in the Pocketguide
- ✓ Create community meetings to educate the public on identity theft
- ✓ Attend existing community meetings to inform the public about identity theft
- ✓ Conduct meetings with local merchants and financial institutions to increase their awareness on identity theft and empower them to be part of your anti-identity theft team

This community meeting conducted by the East Coast Gang Investigators Association focused on Identity Theft and Community Awareness as a Crime Prevention tool

What Personal Items Should be Safeguarded to Stop Identity Theft?

Any personal items that contain information that can help an identity thief create someone's identity for his/her own personal criminal intent. The following items should be safeguarded at all times and when discarded should be thoroughly shredded:

- ✓ Address labels from junk mail and magazines
- ✓ ATM receipts
- ✓ Bank statements and Bank Receipt
- ✓ Birth certificate copies
- ✓ Canceled and voided checks
- ✓ Credit and charge card bills, carbon copies, summaries and receipts
- ✓ Credit applications
- ✓ Credit reports and histories
- ✓ Documents containing maiden name (used by credit card companies for security reasons)
- ✓ Documents containing names, addresses, phone numbers or e-mail addresses
- ✓ Documents relating to investments
- ✓ Documents containing passwords or PIN numbers

- ✓ Driver's licenses or items with a driver's license number
- ✓ Employee pay stubs
- ✓ Employment records
- ✓ Expired passports and visas
- ✓ Identification cards (college IDs, state IDs, employee ID badges, military IDs)
- ✓ Legal documents
- ✓ Investment, stock and property transactions
- ✓ Items with a signature (leases, contracts, letters)
- ✓ Luggage tags
- ✓ Medical and dental records
- ✓ Papers with a Social Security number
- ✓ Passports
- ✓ Pre-approved credit card applications
- ✓ Printed emails or web pages
- ✓ Receipts with checking account numbers
- ✓ Report cards
- ✓ Résumés or curriculum vitae
- ✓ Tax forms
- ✓ Transcripts
- ✓ Travel itineraries
- ✓ Used airline tickets
- ✓ Utility bills (telephone, gas, electric, water, cable TV, Internet)
- ✓ Vehicle registrations, insurance cards, and repair bills

Internet Identity Theft Scams

With the Internet established as a major way we do business, so is it for the Identity Thief. In fact, computer savvy Identity Criminals are able to steal considerably more identity information via the Internet than they can by other means. One informant told the writer of this Pocketguide that when he was in the identity theft business, he sold hundreds of identities each month after obtaining them via hacking into company websites. Besides the traditional way of hacking into computer websites and stealing consumer information, there are a variety of Identity Theft Scams committed each day by identity thieves. Here are some old scams that are still being used by Identity Criminals as well as some new ones:

"Nigerian Email" Scam

This email, also sent to victim's homes in the form of a letter, takes its name from the country of origin of the criminals using this type of scam. While it has been around for several years, it is still being used by identity thieves and larcenists.

FROM: Joy Williams and Kevin Williams,
Reply to: joy_williams7@yahoo.co.uk

DEAR FRIEND,

Permit me to inform you of my desire of entering into business relationship with you. I prayed over it and selected your name among two names due to its esteeming nature and the recommendations given to me as a reputable and trustworthy person I can do business with and by their recommendations I must not hesitate to confide in you for this simple and sincere business.

I am Joy Williams. The daughter of the late Dr. and Mrs. David Williams. My father was a very wealthy cocoa merchant based in Abidjan. The economic capital of Ivory Coast before he was poisoned to death by his business associates, on one of their outing to discuss on a business deal. When my mother died on 21 Oct. 1995. My father took me so special because I am motherless. Before the death of my father on 29th November 2002 in a private hospital here in Abidjan. He secretly called me to his bedside and told me that he has a sum of $12,500.000 US left in a local bank here in Abidjan. He also explained to me that it was because of this wealth that he was poisoned by his business associates and that I should seek a foreign partner in a country of my choice where I will transfer this money and use it for investment purposes. (such as *real estate management]. I am honorably seeking your assistance in the following ways. Can you provide a bank account where this money would be transferred. Can you serve as the guardian of this fund and my younger brother Kevin, who is 20 years old, will make arrangement for us to come to your country to further our education and secure a residential permit in your country. Moreover, I am willing to offer you 20% of the total sum as compensation for your effort after the successful transfer of this fund to your nominated account overseas. Furthermore, you can indicate your option towards assisting me as I believe that this transaction would be concluded within 7 days if you signify interest to assist me. I will appreciate you send me e-mail. I am anticipating to hear from you soon and please do hurry to assist us out here now that this country is in political chaos. We urgently need your kind attention.*

Thanks, and God bless!

Joy and Kevin Williams

"Account Update" Scam

In the past few years, the images of several popular Internet sites, and financial institutions, have been the subject of use by Identity Criminals. Because of the immense popularity of these sites, among Internet users and Internet consumers, their scams were easy to perpetrate. Identity Criminals, savvy to using the Internet and adept at creating computer generated "**Mirror Sites**," which look like the authentic site, send out emails to a multitude of Internet users with links to these popular internet sites such as America Online, Yahoo, eBay, Bank of America and Wells Fargo, to name a few. This spam email scam is also known as *carding* or *phishing*. The purpose is to steal the recipient's identity and account information. These emails contain links to these Mirror Sites that are identical to the real sites, but the link takes the recipient directly to the scam site.

Click Here to Update Your Credit Information

▲

www.AcmeBankScamToStealYourIdentity.com

As you can notice in the above illustration, the **Click Here to Update Your Credit Information** link, when touched by the computer's cursor, shows a URL (*See Glossary for explanation*) to a different Internet address. Most of the time, Internet users never touch the URL to ascertain where the link is taking them.

The fake web page will have a fill-in-the-blank style requesting information like name, address, credit card information, banking accounts, social security numbers, date of birth, and other personal identity information. To add more validity to the fake form, a prominent notice is usually posted such as, *"Never give anyone your password!"* or, *"No one from this organization will ever ask you for your password!"*

The "PayPal Computer Trouble" Scam

Another example of **phishing** and a variation of the Account Update Scam is the PayPal Computer Trouble Email Scam. Thousands of Internet users received an email claiming to come from PayPal, the online consumer payment company. The email claimed there was trouble with their computer system and it had to be shut down. The customers were directed to a fake PayPal website.

Here is the fraudulent site and on the following page is the fill-in report to enter the personal information:

> **PayPal**®
>
> Send Money | Request Money | Shop | Sell
>
> ## Dear PayPal User
>
> Today we had some trouble with one of our computer systems. While the trouble appears to be minor, we are not taking any chances. We decided to take the troubled system offline and replace it with a new system. Unfortunately this caused us to lose some member data. Please follow the link below and log into your account to make sure your information is not affected. Account balances have not been affected.
>
> Because of the inconvenience this causes we are giving all users that repair their missing data their next two incoming transfers for free! You will pay no fees for your next two incoming transfers*.
>
> https://www.paypal.com/cgi-bin/webscr/?cmd=_login-run
>
> Thank you for using PayPal!
>
> * - If fees would normally apply, you will not pay anything for the next two incoming transfers you receive.
>
> PayPal Security
>
> PROTECT YOUR PASSWORD
> NEVER give your password to anyone and ONLY log in at PayPal's website. If anyone asks for your password, please follow the Security Tips instructions on the PayPal website.
>
> About Us | Accounts | Fees | Privacy | Security Center | User Agreement | Developers | Referrals | Help
>
> an eBay company
>
> Copyright © 2002 PayPal. All rights reserved.
> Information about FDIC pass-through insurance

PayPal

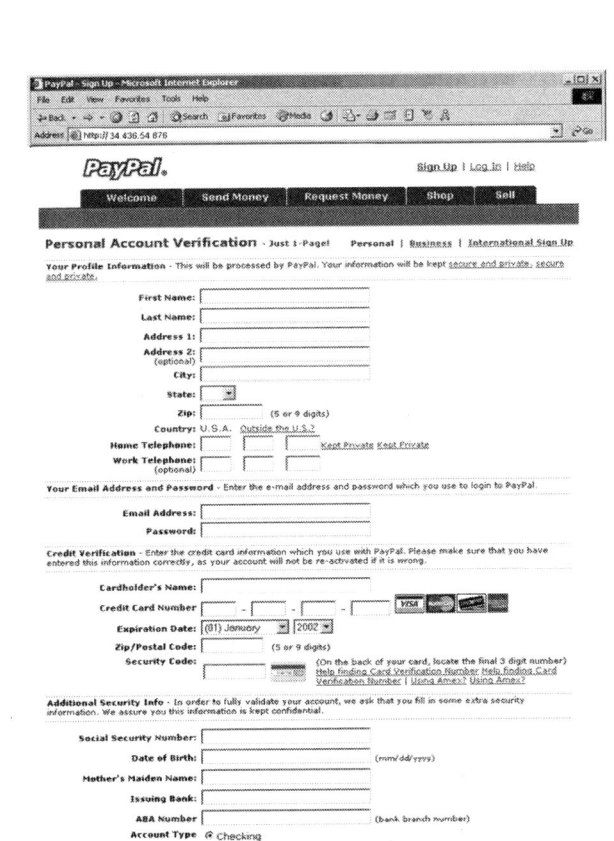

Sign Up | Log In | Help

Welcome | **Send Money** | **Request Money** | **Shop** | **Sell**

Personal Account Verification - Just 1-Page!   Personal | Business | International Sign Up

Your Profile Information - This will be processed by PayPal. Your information will be kept secure and private, secure and private.

- **First Name:**
- **Last Name:**
- **Address 1:**
- **Address 2:** (optional)
- **City:**
- **State:**
- **Zip:** (5 or 9 digits)
- **Country:** U.S.A. Outside the U.S.?
- **Home Telephone:** Kept Private Kept Private
- **Work Telephone:** (optional)

Your Email Address and Password - Enter the e-mail address and password which you use to login to PayPal.

- **Email Address:**
- **Password:**

Credit Verification - Enter the credit card information which you use with PayPal. Please make sure that you have entered this information correctly, as your account will not be re-activated if it is wrong.

- **Cardholder's Name:**
- **Credit Card Number:**   VISA
- **Expiration Date:** (01) January   2002
- **Zip/Postal Code:** (5 or 9 digits)
- **Security Code:** (On the back of your card, locate the final 3 digit number) Help finding Card Verification Number Help finding Card Verification Number | Using Amex? Using Amex?

Additional Security Info - In order to fully validate your account, we ask that you fill in some extra security information. We assure you this information is kept confidential.

- **Social Security Number:**
- **Date of Birth:** (mm/dd/yyyy)
- **Mother's Maiden Name:**
- **Issuing Bank:**
- **ABA Number:** (bank branch number)
- **Account Type:** ● Checking
  ○ Savings
- **Routing Number** ⑁:   ⑁:
  This is the number located between the ⑁ symbols.
- **Account Pin:** (4 digit number * must enter)

"Credit Repair/Credit for those with Poor Credit" Scam

Preying on consumers with poor or limited credit, identity thieves have been sending spam emails across the Internet with the intention of obtaining identity information or, in search of their first credit card or, wanting to repair poor credit, will answer the email and provide information to the bogus credit repair service. The bogus credit repair service steals the identity information from massive amounts of victims and sells it to individual identity thieves and criminals looking to make a quick buck.

"Online Auction" Fraud

The second most reported fraud from consumers to the Federal Trade Commission is Auction Fraud. It totaled 51,000 complaints. Even eBay and Yahoo Auctions have had such crimes committed on their sites. Consumers should look for indications of an auction fraud or scam auction seeking their identity information, such as:

- ✓ Low priced high-ticket items, like high-definition TVs, laptops, or jewelry—especially if there are multiple items for sale
- ✓ Brand-new sellers with no sales history

- ✓ Sellers requesting wire transfers for payment, or payment in foreign currencies
- ✓ Sellers requesting Social Security numbers for tax reporting information
- ✓ Sellers requesting your mother's maiden name
- ✓ Auctions that begin, and end, over a weekend, since eBay customer support is light during those days
- ✓ Seller telephone numbers or addresses that can't be verified

"Fraud Alert Email" Scam

In the late afternoon, on Wednesday, June 18, 2003, several thousand consumers received a fraudulent email labeled **Fraud Alert!,** apparently from Best Buy. This Fraud Alert displayed serious concern over a purchase from one of the Best Buy stores and possible credit card misuse. The email directed the consumers to go to a website to correct the situation. At the website, the consumers were asked to enter their Social Security number and credit card numbers.

Best Buy never sent out such an email and contacted the appropriate authorities immediately. Their computer systems were checked and found to be uncompromised. Customer information was secure. According to Best Buy

Public Relations, two fraudulent websites have been shut down to date.

The full story can be accessed on the Best Buy website in the news Archive section by going to:

http://communications.bestbuy.com/pressroom/Archive.asp

or by calling Best Buy Customer Care: 888-BEST-BUY

"Identity Theft Protection" Scam

The Federal Trade Commission warns that some companies, sending emails and making telephone calls, to consumers, claim to be identity theft prevention services, when, in fact, they are identity criminals. They are trying to get the consumer's driver's license number, mother's maiden name, Social Security number, credit card information, and bank account numbers.

"You Have Won a Prize" Scam

While everyone likes to win a prize, a free gift, a sweepstakes, or a raffle, they should be very wary of an email, telephone call or a letter offering a chance to receive such prizes with the requirement of giving out personal data. This data, such as a Social Security number, credit card number or expiration date, or mother's maiden name, is just another scam to steal someone's identity.

"Make $$$ Stuffing Envelopes" Scam

These business opportunities make it sound easy to start a business that will bring lots of income without much work or cash outlay. The solicitations trumpet unbelievable earnings claims of $140 a day, $1,000 a day, or more, and claim that the business doesn't involve selling, meetings, or personal contact with others, or that someone else will do all the work. Many business opportunity solicitations claim to offer a way to make money in an Internet-related business.

Short on details but long on promises, these messages usually offer a telephone number to call for more information. In many cases, you'll be told to leave your name and telephone number so that a salesperson can call you back with the sales pitch. Of course, in order to start in the business, you'll have to provide some personal data and a credit card account or bank account. NOT!

Collecting Evidence in Identity Theft Cases

As in every criminal investigation, collecting evidence is extremely important to its progress and hopeful success. While identity theft is difficult to identify, the success of any investigation will rely on three stages of evidence that must be collected.

Stage 1: Copies of Initial reports indicating identity theft has occurred and affidavits from the victim (See Identity Theft Affidavit). These reports can include letters from financial institutions indicating a debt or a simple notification of the victim's account compromised as well as Credit Reports (see Using a Credit Report to Identify Identity Theft).

Stage 2: A profile of the victim which includes the victim's description, photograph, and signature sample. This will be used to show bank tellers and store clerks how to establish that the victim is not the person who has used the identity documents and credit instruments (credit cards, checks, etc…) during the crime. This will also aid in those cases where identity theft is falsely reported.

Stage 3: Original documents generated by the Identity Thief including credit applications, signature cards, US Postal Service change of address cards, credit cards (seized or provided by the identity theft victim) or any document used to further the identity theft.

The Identity Theft Crime Scene

The mere concept of a crime scene, when it comes to identity theft, seems ludicrous, but, like every single crime committed identity theft has its own crime scene. Whether the crime of identity theft has occurred as a result of internet fraud or dumpster diving, and the subsequent crimes may occur at a store or a financial institution for the purpose of financial gain, there will be a scene of the crime to process.

Unless it is specifically known when, how and where the identity crime was perpetrated, and the scene of the crime is intact, conventional crime scene processing, such as photographing or dusting for fingerprints, will be rare or nonexistent. When computer-related identity thefts occur, the crime scene will be the computer and quite possibly the Internet. Latent traces (on the computer hard drive) of Internet Sites accessed could lead to identifying an identity theft crime scene. A computer forensic specialist should be used when the investigator does not have the computer savvy to uncover such information on the victim's computer. For basic computer searches for this information, the following procedure can be followed to uncover all sites (accessed) listed in the computer's Internet History.

> **Internet History Procedure:** *After the computer is turned on and completely booted, place the cursor on the **START** button and right click. Left click on **EXPLORE**. Left click on **TEMPORARY INTERNET FILES.*** Left click on **HISTORY** to access the window listing all the Internet sites accessed that are still on the computer hard drive. These sites can be copied, pasted into a word document, and printed out or saved to a disk.

To identify those Internet sites that have left a cookie (electronic trace) to the victim's computer, follow this next procedure.

> **Internet Site Cookie Procedure:** *After the computer is turned on and completely booted, place the cursor on the **START** button and right click. After left clicking on **EXPLORE**, left click on **COOKIES*** to access the window listing all the Internet sites that sent a cookie to the computer hard drive. These sites can be copied, pasted into a word document, and printed out or saved to a disk.

Using Credit Reports to Spot Identity Theft

A person's credit report can offer a lot of information should the crime of identity theft occur. It can also be a prevention tool when reviewed often by a trained eye. Specific aspects of the credit report are the best and easiest way of indicating an identity theft. The sections of a credit report that a consumer should pay close attention to, are:

- ✓ **Address:** Usually at the beginning of a credit report is the consumer's current address, previous address, and other addresses used. Addresses unfamiliar to the consumer, could be an indication that an identity thief has filed a change of address form redirecting credit cards or bank statements to the identity thief's safe house or mail drop or that a thief has obtained credit cards in the consumer's name, and the credit card company is sending correspondence to the other address.

- ✓ **Credit Rating:** A low credit rating, when the consumer knows he/she has been promptly paying bills can be an indication there is a problem within the credit report. The problems that can cause a poor credit rating may be from credit card bills left unpaid because an identity thief has obtained credit cards in the consumer's name.

- ✓ **Derogatory Activity:** This is usually an indication of delinquent accounts that are not being paid, or being paid late.

- ✓ **Inquiries by:** This section indicates which companies or creditors have done a credit inquiry on the consumer recently. The consumer should become alarmed when these inquiries are made and the consumer is unaware of any transaction with such companies. If an identity thief is using the consumer's identity to obtain credit, a cell phone account, or applying for a loan, there will be an inquiry by one of the companies into the credit.

- ✓ **Fraud Alert:** A consumer can place a fraud alert on his/her account to be notified of any suspicious activity generated by an inquiry into the credit report. When being notified of a Fraud Alert without making any credit related transactions, the consumer should immediately become suspicious and investigate the cause of the alert.

- ✓ **Installment Balance:** When an installment balance is different than the consumer's records indicate, an immediate investigation should be conducted by the consumer to ascertain the problem and if an identity crime has occurred, the police should be contacted.

Any suspicious activity on a credit report should be thoroughly investigated immediately. Spotting identity theft early may save the consumer years of credit headaches.

Your Credit Report Company
www.creditreport4U.com
1-800-Credit4U

Report Date: 8/29/03 **Reference #:** 1-23-567-8
Name: Doe, John   **Soc. Sec. #:** SSN Provided

Address: 1234 Washington Avenue, Anytown, USA
Former Address: 710 Union Street, Pleasantville, CA
Other Address:

Oldest Account: Amex 5453xxxxxxxxxxxx

Account Name/Number/Type of Account
Cred Date High Mthly Acct Last Acct Past Last
Bur Open Limit Pymt Bal Rptd Status Due Delq

AMEX REVOLVING 5453XXXX
(01) 10-00 1310 25 866 07-03 Curr (30) 1 xx

SEARS REVOLVING 6787XXXX
(03) 12-97 4000 261 3718 06-03 Curr (30) 1 xx

PUBLIC RECORD INFORMATION
Chapter 7 Bankruptcy Filed 03-95
Chapter 7 Bankruptcy Discharged 07-95

RECENT INQUIRIES ON THIS ACCOUNT
Acme Auto Dealer 5-19-03
MBNA Bank Credit 4-13-03
Sprint Cellular 6-06-03

NOTES

Frequently Asked Questions

What do I do if my checks or bank account information were stolen?

Close your bank account. Open a new one with a new account number. Tell the bank you want to use a new password for access to your new account. Do not use your mother's maiden name or the last four digits of your Social Security number. Report the stolen checks to the check verification companies that stores use. For more information on stolen checks, see *Identity Theft: What to Do When It Happens to You*, at:

www.privacyrights.org/fs/fs17a.htm

What do I do if my driver's license, learner's permit, or Motor Vehicles Department issued ID card was stolen?

Immediately contact your local DMV office to report the theft. Ask them to put a fraud alert on your license. If the thief is using your license as ID, you may want to change your license number. Ask DMV for an appointment. Take a copy of the police report and copies of bills or other items supporting your claim of fraud. You will also need to prove your identity. Take current documents such as a passport, a certification of citizenship or naturalization, or a U.S. military photo ID. DMV will issue a new driver's license or ID card number when you meet all the requirements. For more information, see *Identity Theft: Have You Been A Victim of Identity Theft? DMV Can Help*, available at:

www.dmv.ca.gov/pubs/brochures/fast_facts/
   ffdl24.htm

What do I do if my mail was stolen or my address was changed by the identity thief?

Notify the Postal Inspector if you think the identity thief has stolen your mail or filed a change of address request in your name. To find your nearest Postal Inspector, look in the white pages of the telephone book for the Post Office listing under United States Government, or go to the Postal Inspection Service's web site at:

www.usps.gov/websites/depart/inspect

What do I do if I am wrongly accused of a crime committed by an identity thief?

In the case of a false civil judgment, contact the court where the judgment was entered. Report that you are a victim of identity theft. In the case of a false criminal judgment, contact the local US Attorney's Office and the FBI. Ask them for information on how to clear your name. To find the local field office of the FBI, look in the white pages of the telephone book for the FBI under United States Government, or go to the FBI's web site at:

www.fbi.gov/contact/fo/fo.htm

What do I do if I am contacted by a debt collector?

Tell the debt collector that you are the victim of identity theft. Say that you dispute the validity of the debt. Say that you did not create the debt and are not responsible for it. Send the collector a follow-up letter saying the same things. Include a copy of your police report and of any documents you've received from the creditor. Write that your letter gives notice that a situation of identity theft exists. Send the letter by certified mail, return receipt requested. If the debt collector is not the original creditor, send your letter within 30 days of receiving the collector's first written demand for payment.

What if I think my Social Security number is being used?

Sometimes, an identity thief will use the victim's Social Security (SS) number to be able to work. It's a good idea to check your Social Security earnings record to see if the thief is using your SS number. You can get a copy of your earnings record by calling 1-800-772-1213, or get a Request for Social Security Statement (Form 7004) at www.ssa.gov/online/ssa-7004.pdf. If the thief is using your SS number, call the Social Security Fraud Hotline at 1-800-269-0271. You can also read, *When Someone Misuses Your Number*, at:

www.ssa.gov/pubs/10064.html

What a Victim of Identity Theft Must Do Immediately!

1. Report the fraud to the 3 major credit bureaus

Ask each of the credit bureaus to flag your file with a **fraud alert**. Also, ask them to add a victim's statement to your credit report. The victim's statement tells creditors to call you to get your approval if they receive requests to open new accounts. Give them a phone number to use to contact you. Ask each credit bureau for a free copy of your credit report. As a victim of identity theft, you have the right to a free report from each credit bureau. For more on what to tell the credit bureaus, see *Identity Theft: What to Do When It Happens to You*, at:

www.privacyrights.org/fs/fs17a.htm

2. Make a police report

Under the law of most states, you can report identity theft to your local police department. Ask the police to issue a police report of identity theft. You may have to show copies of the laws to the police. The laws are on the last pages of this information sheet. Give the police as much information on the theft as possible. Give them any new evidence you collect to add to your report. Be sure to get a copy of your police report. You will need to give copies to creditors and the credit bureaus. For more information, see *Organizing Your Identity Theft Case* by the Identity Theft Resource Center, available at:

www.privacyrights.org/fs/fs17b-org.htm

3. Request information on fraudulent accounts

When you file your police report of identity theft, the officer may give you forms to use to request account information from credit grantors. If the officer does not do this, you can use the forms available from the Office of Privacy Protection at:

www.privacyprotection.ca.gov/cover/identitytheft.htm

Send copies of the forms to all creditors where the thief opened or applied for accounts, along with copies of the police report as described below. Give the information you receive from creditors to the investigating officer.

4. Call all the creditors

Call all creditors for any accounts that the thief opened or used. When you call, ask for the security or fraud department. Creditors can be credit card companies, other lenders, phone companies, other utility companies, and department stores. Tell them you are an identity theft victim. Ask them not to hold you responsible for charges the thief made. Ask them to close those accounts and to report them to credit bureaus as "closed at consumer's request." If you open new accounts, have them set up to require a password or PIN to approve use. Don't use your mother's maiden name or the last four numbers of your Social Security number as your password. For more information on what to tell creditors, see the Federal Trade Commission's *When Bad Things Happen to Your Good Name*, available at:

www.ftc.gov/bcp/conline/pubs/credit/idtheft.htm

5. Review your credit reports carefully

Look for accounts opened in your name that you did not open. Also, look for charges to your accounts that you did not make. And look for late payments or non-payments that are not yours. Check your name, address and Social Security number. Look at the Inquiries section of the report. Ask the credit bureaus to remove any inquiries from companies holding fraudulent accounts in your name. Ask each credit bureau to remove all information in your credit report that results from the theft. Order new credit reports every three months until your situation has cleared up. You may have to pay $8 for each report after the first free one.

6. Use the ID Theft Affidavit

The Federal Trade Commission's ID Theft Affidavit is a form that can help you clear up your records. (*See the form in the chapter entitled, Identity Theft Affidavit*) The Affidavit is accepted by the credit bureaus and by many major creditors. Send copies of the completed form to creditors where the thief opened accounts in your name. Also send copies to creditors where the thief made charges on your account, to the credit bureaus, and to the police. The form is available on the FTC web site at:

www.consumer.gov/idtheft

7. Write to the credit bureaus

Write a letter to each credit bureau. Repeat what you said in your telephone call (see above). Send copies of your police report and completed ID Theft Affidavit. Remind the credit bureaus that they must remove any information that you, an identity theft victim, say is the result of the theft. Send your letters by certified mail, return receipt requested. Keep a copy of each letter.

8. Write to your creditors

Write a letter to each creditor. Repeat what you said in your telephone call (see above). Send copies of your police report and the completed ID Theft Affidavit. Send your letters by certified mail, return receipt requested. Keep copies of your letters. Continue to review your bills carefully and report any new fraudulent charges to the creditor.

State Laws Pertaining to Identity Theft

The following is a listing of State laws pertaining to identity theft listed by the respective state. States that are not listed do not have a specific law dealing with identity theft (as of this writing) but each state has a law(s) applicable to the crimes relating to identity theft that will insure the sufficient protection to victims.

Alabama	Alabama Code § 13A-8-190 through 201
Alaska	Alaska Stat. § 11.46.565
Arizona	Ariz. Rev. Stat. § 13-2008
Arkansas	Ark. Code Ann. § 5-37-227
California	Cal. Penal Code § 530.5-8
Colorado	No specific ID Theft law.
Connecticut	CT. Stat. § 53a-129a (criminal)
	CT. Stat. § 52-571h (civil)
Delaware	Del. Code Ann. Title 11, § 854
District of Columbia	No specific ID Theft law.
Florida	Fla. Stat. Ann. § 817.568
Georgia	Ga. Code Ann. § 16-9-120
	Through 128
Hawaii	HI Rev. Stat. § 708-839.6-8
Idaho	Idaho Code § 18-3126 (criminal)
	Idaho Code 28-51-102 (civil)
Illinois	720 Ill. Comp. Stat. 5/16 G

Indiana	Ind. Code § 35-43-5-3.5
Iowa	Iowa Code § 715A.8 (criminal)
	Iowa Code § 714.16.B (civil)
Kansas	Kan. Stat. Ann. § 21-4018
Kentucky	Ky. Rev. Stat. Ann. § 514.160
Louisiana	La. Rev. Stat. Ann. §14:67.16
Maine	ME Rev. Stat. Ann. Title 17-A § 905-A
Maryland	Md. Code Ann. Art. 27 § 231
Massachusetts	Mass. Gen. Laws Ch. 266, § 37E
Michigan	Mich. Comp. Laws § 750.285
Minnesota	Minn. Stat. Ann. § 609.527
Mississippi	Miss. Code Ann. § 97-19-85
Missouri	Mo. Rev. Stat. § 570.223
Montana	Mon. Code Ann. § 45-6-332
Nebraska	NE Rev. Stat. § 28-608 and 620
Nevada	Nev. Rev. State. § 205.463
	Through 465
New Hampshire	N.H. Rev. Stat. Ann. § 638:26
New Jersey	N.J. Stat. Ann. § 2C:21-17
New Mexico	N.M. Stat. Ann. § 30-16-24.1
New York	NY Penal Law § 190.77
	Through 190.84
North Carolina	N.C. Gen. Stat. § 14-113.20
	Through 23
North Dakota	N.D.C.C. § 12.1-23-11
Ohio	Ohio Rev. Code Ann. § 2913.49

Oklahoma	Okla. Stat. Title 21, § 1533.1
Oregon	Or. Rev. Stat. § 165.800
Pennsylvania	18 Pa. Cons. State § 4120
Rhode Island	R.I. Gen. Laws § 11-49.1-1
South Carolina	S.C. Code Ann. § 16-13-500, 501
South Dakota	S.D. Codified Laws § 22-30A-3.1.
Tennessee	TCA § 39-14-150 (criminal)
	TCA § 47-18-2101 (civil)
Texas	Tex. Penal Code § 32.51
Utah	Utah Code Ann. § 76-6-1101-1104
Vermont	No specific ID Theft law.
Virginia	Va. Code Ann. § 18.2-186.3
Washington	Wash. Rev. Code § 9.35.020
West Virginia	W. Va. Code § 61-3-54
Wisconsin	Wis. Stat. § 943.201
Wyoming	Wyo. Stat. Ann. § 6-3-901

U.S. Territories

Guam	9 Guam Code Ann. § 46.80
U.S. Virgin Islands	No specific ID Theft law.

Federal Laws Pertaining to Identity Theft

Identity Theft and Assumption Deterrence Act
18 U.S.C. § 1028

In October, 1998, Congress passed the Identity Theft and Assumption Deterrence Act of 1998 (Identity Theft Act) to address the problem of identity theft. Specifically, the Act amended 18 U.S.C. § 1028 to make it a federal crime when anyone knowingly transfers or uses, without lawful authority, a means of identification of another person with the intent to commit, or to aid or abet, any unlawful activity that constitutes a violation of Federal law, or that constitutes a felony under any applicable State or local law.

www.ftc.gov/bcp/conline/pubs/credit/affidavit.pdf

Other Federal Laws:

Fair Credit Reporting Act   15 U.S.C. § 1681
The Fair Credit Reporting Act establishes procedures for correcting mistakes on your credit record and requires that your record only be provided for legitimate business needs.

Fair Credit Billing Act
The Fair Credit Billing Act establishes procedures for resolving billing errors on your credit card accounts. It also limits a consumer's liability for fraudulent credit card charges.

Fair Debt Collection Practices Act
The Fair Debt Collection Practices Act prohibits debt collectors from using unfair or deceptive practices to collect overdue bills that your creditor has forwarded for collection.

Electronic Fund Transfer Act
The Electronic Fund Transfer Act provides consumer protection for all transactions using a debit card or electronic means to debit or credit an account. It also limits a consumer's liability for unauthorized electronic fund transfers.

Identity Theft Affidavit

Victim Information

(1) My full legal name is _____
      (First)   (Middle)   (Last)   (Jr., Sr., III)

(2) (If different from above) When the events described in this affidavit took place, I was known as

_____
(First)   (Middle)   (Last)   (Jr., Sr., III)

(3) My date of birth is _____
      (day/month/year)

(4) My social security number is _____

(5) My driver's license or identification card state and number are _____

(6) My current address is _____

City _____ State _____ Zip Code _____

(7) I have lived at this address since _____
      (month/year)

(8) (If different from above) When the events described in this affidavit took place, my address

was _____

City _____ State _____ Zip Code _____

(9) I lived at the address in #8 from _____ until _____
      (month/year) (month/year)

(10) My daytime telephone number is (___) _____

My evening telephone number is (___) _____

How the Fraud Occurred

Check all that apply for items 11 - 17:

(11) ☐ I did not authorize anyone to use my name or personal information to seek the money, credit, loans, goods or services described in this report.

(12) ☐ I did not receive any benefit, money, goods or services as a result of the events described in this report.

(13) ☐ My identification documents (for example, credit cards; birth certificate; driver's license; social security card; etc.) were ☐ stolen   ☐ lost on or about _____.
                                                                                         (day/month/year)

(14) ☐ To the best of my knowledge and belief, the following person(s) used my information (for example, my name, address, date of birth, existing account numbers, social security number, mother's maiden name, etc.) or identification documents to get money, credit, loans, goods or services without my knowledge or authorization:

Name (if known)	Name (if known)
Address (if known)	Address (if known)
Phone number(s) (if known)	Phone number(s) (if known)
additional information (if known)	additional information (if known)

(15) ☐ I do NOT know who used my information or identification documents to get money, credit, loans, goods or services without my knowledge or authorization.

(16) ☐ Additional comments: (For example, description of the fraud, which documents or information were used or how the identity thief gained access to your information.)

_____
_____
_____
_____
_____

(Attach additional pages as necessary.)

Victim's Law Enforcement Actions

(17) (check one) I ☐ am ☐ am not willing to assist in the prosecution of the person(s) who committed this fraud.

(18) (check one) I ☐ am ☐ am not authorizing the release of this information to law enforcement for the purpose of assisting them in the investigation and prosecution of the person(s) who committed this fraud.

(19) (check all that apply) I ☐ have ☐ have not reported the events described in this affidavit to the police or other law enforcement agency. The police ☐ did ☐ did not write a report.
In the event you have contacted the police or other law enforcement agency, please complete the following:

(Agency #1)	(Officer/Agency personnel taking report)
(Date of report)	(Report Number, if any)
(Phone number)	(e-mail address, if any)
(Agency #2)	(Officer/Agency personnel taking report)
(Date of report)	(Report Number, if any)
(Phone number)	(e-mail address, if any)

Documentation Checklist

Please indicate the supporting documentation you are able to provide to the companies you plan to notify. Attach copies (NOT originals) to the affidavit before sending it to the companies.

(20) ☐ A copy of a valid government-issued photo-identification card (for example, your driver's license, state-issued ID card or your passport). If you are under 16 and don't have a photo-ID, you may submit a copy of your birth certificate or a copy of your official school records showing your enrollment and place of residence.

(21) ☐ Proof of residency during the time the disputed bill occurred, the loan was made or the other event took place (for example, a rental/lease agreement in your name, a copy of a utility bill or a copy of an insurance bill).

(22) ☐ A copy of the report you filed with the police or sheriff's department. If you are unable to obtain a report or report number from the police, please indicate that in Item 19. Some companies only need the report number, not a copy of the report. You may want to check with each company.

Signature

I declare under penalty of perjury that the information I have provided in this affidavit is true and correct to the best of my knowledge.

_____   _____
(signature)   (date signed)

Knowingly submitting false information on this form could subject you to criminal prosecution for perjury.

_____
(Notary)

[Check with each company. Creditors sometimes require notarization. If they do not, please have one witness (non-relative) sign below that you completed and signed this affidavit.]

Witness:

_____   _____
(signature)   (printed name)

_____   _____
(date)   (telephone number)

Fraudulent Account Statement

> **Completing this Statement**
> - Make as many copies of this page as you need. **Complete a separate page for each company you're notifying and only send it to that company.** Include a copy of your signed affidavit.
> - List only the account(s) you're disputing with the company receiving this form. **See the example below.**
> - If a collection agency sent you a statement, letter or notice about the fraudulent account, attach a copy of that document (**NOT** the original).

I declare (check all that apply):

☐ As a result of the event(s) described in the ID Theft Affidavit, the following account(s) was/were opened at your company in my name without my knowledge, permission or authorization using my personal information or identifying documents:

Creditor Name/Address *(the company that opened the account or provided the goods or services)*	Account Number	Type of unauthorized credit/goods/services provided by creditor *(if known)*	Date issued or opened *(if known)*	Amount/Value provided *(the amount charged or the cost of the goods/services)*
Example Example National Bank 22 Main Street Columbus, Ohio 22722	01234567-89	auto loan	01/05/2000	$25,500.00

☐ During the time of the accounts described above, I had the following account open with your company:

Billing name _____

Identity Theft Fact Sheet

This fact sheet is for informational purposes and should not be construed as legal advice or as policy of any government office. Readers desiring advice in particular cases should consult an attorney or other expert. The fact sheet may be copied, if (1) the meaning of the copied text is not changed or misrepresented, (2) credit is given to the Office of Privacy Protection, and (3) all copies are distributed free of charge.

Calls to Credit Bureaus

Credit Bureau	Date	Contact Person	Comments
Equifax 800-525-6285			
Experian 888-397-3742			
Trans Union 800-680-7289			

Calls to Police

Date	Contact Person	Comments

Calls to Creditors

Creditor	Date	Contact Person	Comments

Letters to Credit Bureaus

Credit Bureau	Date Sent
Equifax P. O. Box 740241 Atlanta, GA 30374	
Experian Consumer Fraud Assistance P. O. Box 949 Allen, TX 75013	
Trans Union Fraud Victim Assistance Division P. O. Box 6790 Fullerton, CA 92834	

Letters to Creditors

Creditor	Date Sent

Remember to keep copies of all letters!

Calls to Check Verification Companies

Company	Phone Number	Date	Contact Person	Comments
CheckRite	800-766-2748			
Chexsystems	800-428-9623			
CrossCheck	800-843-0760			
Equifax	800-437-5120			
SCAN	800-262-7771			
Telecheck	800-710-9898			
International Check Services	800-526-5380			

Dispute Letter

Sample Dispute Letter — Credit Bureau

Date
Your Name
Your Address
Your City, State, Zip Code

Complaint Department
Name of Credit Bureau
Address
City, State, Zip Code
Dear Sir or Madam:

I am writing to dispute the following information in my file. The items I dispute also are circled on the attached copy of the report I received. (Identify item(s) disputed by name of source, such as creditors or tax court, and identify type of item, such as credit account, judgment, etc.)

This item is (inaccurate or incomplete) because (describe what is inaccurate or incomplete and why). I am requesting that the item be deleted (or request another specific change) to correct the information.

Enclosed are copies of (use this sentence if applicable and describe any enclosed documentation, such as payment records, court documents) documentation supporting my position. Please investigate this (these) matter(s) and (delete or correct) the disputed item(s) as soon as possible.

Sincerely, Your name

Enclosures: (List what you are enclosing.)

Sample Dispute Letter — Credit Card Issuers

Date

Your Name
Your Address
Your City, State, Zip Code
Your Account Number
Name of Creditor
Billing Inquiries
Address
City, State, Zip Code

Dear Sir or Madam:

I am writing to dispute a billing error in the amount of $_____ on my account. The amount is inaccurate because (describe the problem). I am requesting that the error be corrected, that any finance and other charges related to the disputed amount be credited as well, and that I receive an accurate statement.

Enclosed are copies of (use this sentence to describe any enclosed information, such as sales slips, payment records) supporting my position. Please investigate this matter and correct the billing error as soon as possible.

Sincerely,

Your name

Enclosures: (List what you are enclosing.)

Crime Prevention Tips to Stop Identity Theft

The following crime prevention suggestions will help citizens avoid becoming a victim of identity theft as well as *recognizing an identity theft crime in the early stages.*

1. Limit the number of identifying documents you carry on your person.

2. Give out your Social Security number only when it is absolutely necessary, but ask if other types of identification can be used in its place.

3. Before revealing any personal and valuable information, find out what it is going to be used for and whether it is going to be shared with others.

4. When using your credit card in restaurants or stores, keep an eye on the credit card and the clerk at all times. Be aware of the Swipe Theft and Credit Card Skimmers.

5. Be cognizant of the 'Overhear' method or 'Shoulder Surf', method of someone listening in to your conversation or peering over your shoulder to obtain your credit card numbers,

check numbers, telephone numbers, social security numbers, or any other information that may be useful to a criminal bent on perpetrating an Identity related theft.

6. Keep items, at home or at work, in a secure place, especially if you share a residence or office with others. Keep the items secure from cleaning services and others who have access to your residence or office.

7. Ascertain who has access to your personal information and if it is kept in a secure place.

8. Get into a habit of shredding all credit card receipts, bank statements, financial statements and any other papers listing your credit card numbers or other financial information.

9. Obliterate or thoroughly cut old credit cards or any other old membership cards into many pieces so the numbers and magnetic strips can't be read.

10. Protect your paychecks and check stubs since many employers place the employee's social security number on the check or stub.

11. Protect your employee ID cards since many employers use the employee's social security number as the employee ID number.

12. Put passwords on credit cards, bank accounts and phone accounts.

13. Thoroughly destroy anything you throw out. Criminals obtain much valuable and useful information from your trash can.

14. Use only secure Web sites from trusted companies for Internet purchases.

15. Be careful when speaking on cordless or cellular telephones and avoid discussing financial issues.

16. Don't give out personal information over the phone or Internet unless you initiated the contact or know who you are dealing with.

17. Visit, write, or call your local Department of Motor Vehicles to have your personal information protected from disclosure.

18. Avoid using easily available information such as your mother's maiden name, telephone number, or last four digits of your Social Security number

as a password on your credit cards or banking accounts.

19. Be suspicious of someone calling to confirm personal information.

20. Do not answer any letter that says you will get a large amount of money if you can "help me set up a bank account."

21. Be suspicious of any email requesting your password or personal information. Internet Service Providers do not ask this type of information after initial account activation.

22. Be suspicious of emails from Internet companies such as eBay, Yahoo and America Online, there are thousands of reports of Internet scams using fake sites that appear almost identical to these major companies.

23. Be suspicious of scams via the Internet such as 'Account Update', 'Fraud Protection', 'Identity Theft Protection', 'You have just Won', or any Internet message. Check with the proper companies before answering any email or alert asking for your personal information.

24. Thoroughly review all bank, credit card and phone statements for unusual activity.

25. Be cognizant of the dates and time frames when new credit cards or checks are being mailed to you and quickly report any that are missing or late.

26. Pay attention to billing cycles. Missing credit card bills could be an indication an identity theft has occurred. An Identity criminal may have obtained your bill, used another address, and is using your bill to perpetrate a crime.

27. Reduce the number of pre-approved credit card offers you will receive by calling **888-5OPTOUT**

28. Get into a habit of taking your mail in promptly after delivery and install a secure mail box for your mail to be delivered to. Mail theft is common today and a popular place for identity theft to start.

29. Do not leave outgoing credit card payments or mail in your mailbox for pick-up. Make a delivery to the Post Office personally.

30. Don't leave valuable identity information in your hotel room while out on the town or conducting

business out of your hotel room. Even top-rated hotels can be prone to a dishonest maid or hotel employee that may have occasion to enter your room and steal identity information such as credit card numbers, social security numbers, date of birth, etc…

31. Close all unused credit and bank accounts and carefully obliterate or shred unused credit card offers.

32. Have your Social Security number removed from checks, driver's licenses or other identification.

33. Get into a habit of asking for the carbon papers of credit purchases.

34. Maintain a record of Credit purchases, loan applications and store credit request applications.

35. Don't carry your Social Security card in your wallet unless it is needed. Memorize it!

36. If you're traveling, have your mail held at your local post office, or ask someone you know well and trust, another family member, a friend, or a neighbor to collect and hold your mail while you're away.

37. If you have to telephone someone while you're traveling, and need to pass on personal financial information to the person you're calling, don't do it at an open telephone booth where passersby can listen in on what you're saying; use a telephone booth where you can close the door, or wait until you're at a less public location to call.

38. Order a credit report a few times a year from any of the Credit Reporting Companies as well as a complete Credit Card Report at least once a year. Analyze the reports for unusual or unfamiliar activity and question suspicious charges and activities.

39. Pay attention to mistakes on your identity items (Social Security Cards, Driver's Licenses, Credit Cards, Checking Accounts, etc...) such as misspellings, wrong addresses, missing initials, wrong phone numbers or any other mistake, because these mistakes may be an indication that someone, other than you, has stolen your identity.

40. Pay attention to mistakes on your credit reports and your banking statements. This may be an indication that someone has already victimized you.

Resources for Prevention & Investigation

Government Guide: ID Theft

A *Governmentguide* web site providing information, statistics and prevention suggestions regarding identity theft.

www.governmentguide.com/consumer_services/idtheft.adp

Credit Reporting Companies

TransUnion

800-888-4213 or www.tuc.com
Fraud Division – **800-680-7289**

Experian

888-EXPERIAN or www.experian.com
Fraud Division – **888-397-3742**

Equifax

800-685-1111 or www.equifax.com
Fraud Division – **800-525-6285**

Consumer & Victim Assistance

Identity Theft Resource Center

P.O. Box 26833, San Diego, CA 92126

The Identity Theft Resource Center is a nonprofit organization specializing in identity theft and victim assistance. **858-693-7935**

www.idtheftcenter.org

Social Security Administration ID Theft Hotline

The Social Security Administration maintains an ID Theft Hotline that can be reached at **800-269-0271** or online.

www.ssa.gov/oig

California Department of Consumer Affairs

Office of Privacy Protection
400 R Street, Suite 3000
Sacramento, CA 95814
(866) 785-9663 (in California only)
(916) 445-1254

www.privacy.ca.gov
privacy@dca.ca.gov

Privacy Rights Clearinghouse

3100 5th Avenue, Suite B, San Diego, CA 92103

A Nonprofit organization specializing in privacy and ID theft. **619-298-3396**

www.privacyrights.org

Federal Trade Commission

The Federal Trade Commission operates an Identity Theft Clearinghouse. You can order free copies of *When Bad Things Happen to Your Good Name* to give to victims of identity theft. The FTC's ID theft database statistics can be found at www.consumer.gov/sentinel. Your agency might want to become a member of its Sentinel program. **877-IDTHEFT**

www.consumer.gov/idtheft

Public Interest Research Group

The Public Interest Research Group is a consumer advocacy organization that has worked on the ID theft issue for many years, advocating stronger laws.

www.pirg.org and www.calpirg.org

Reducing Unsolicited Credit Card Applications

Reduce the number of credit card applications received in the mail. They will, however, ask for a person's Social Security number.

Call: 888-5OPT-OUT

To Make Complaints Against Financial Institutions

If you think a financial institution or company has failed to fulfill its responsibilities to you under the **Electronic Fund Transfer Act**, Speak Up. In addition, you may wish to complain to the appropriate federal agency listed below that has enforcement jurisdiction over that company.

Complaint about a: **State Member Bank of the Federal Reserve System**

Write to: Consumer and Community Affairs
Board of Governors of the Fed. Res. System
20th & C Streets, NW, Mail Stop 801
Washington, DC 20551

www.federalreserve.gov

Complaint about a: **National Bank**

Write to: Office of the Comptroller of the Currency
Compliance Management
Mail Stop 7-5
Washington, DC 20219

www.occ.treas.gov

Complaint about a: **Federal Credit Union**

Write to: National Credit Union Administration
1775 Duke Street
Alexandria, VA 22314

www.ncua.gov

Complaint about a: **Non-Member Federally Insured Bank**

Write to: Office of Consumer Programs
Federal Deposit Insurance Corporation
550 17th Street, NW
Washington, DC 20429

www.fdic.gov

Complaint about a: **Federally Insured Savings and Loan, or Federally Chartered State Bank**

Write to: Consumer Affairs Program
Office of Thrift Supervision
1700 G Street, NW
Washington, DC 20552

www.ots.treas.gov

Federal Trade Commission's Consumer Sentinel

www.consumer.gov/sentinel/index.html

You can get facts on consumer frauds, Internet cons, prize promotions scams, work-at-home schemes, telemarketing scams and identity theft. You can report fraud complaints so they can be shared with law enforcement officials across the U.S. and around the world, and learn how U.S., Canadian, and Australian law enforcers work together with private sector companies and consumer organizations to combat fraud. You can even see trends, and the types of complaints consumers file.

Consumer Sentinel members include more than 700 law enforcement agencies in Australia, Canada and the United States. It helps them build cases and detect trends in consumer fraud and identity theft. Consumer Sentinel gives law enforcers access to over one million complaints including consumer complaints from numerous Better Business Bureaus, the National Fraud Information Center, and Canada's PhoneBusters.

NOTES

Glossary of Terms and Definitions

Account Update Scam: An internet email scam that sends emails to customers of Internet Service Providers, Online Stores and other consumer business with a link to a fake but identical web page with a request for an account update for the purpose of stealing financial and identity information.

Barcode Reader: A handheld scanner used to read the barcode on identification cards and drivers' licenses that is sometimes used by identity thieves to steal the personal information of a victim.

Bust Out: A credit card scam, common among Middle Eastern criminals, in which credit cards are obtained in the name of deported persons or associates, so the criminals can charge on the credit cards to the maximum amount with no intention of paying the bill.

Carding: See *Phishing*

Chat Room Scam: A scam in which an identity thief enters chat rooms with the intention of gathering identity information.

Credit Card Skimmer: A device used to secretly swipe a credit card through in order to steal the account information. Also known as a Skimmer or Swipe Tool.

Credit Card Theft: A theft of a credit card, usually by stealing the mail.

Creditor: A company that issues credit.

Credit Repair Scam: An email, letter, or telephone solicitation to a consumer in an attempt to steal identity information.

Crosscut Shredder: A mechanical paper shredder that cuts paper vertically and horizontally to insure safety from criminals who rummage through garbage to piece together valuable identity information.

Dumpster Diving: A term used to describe rummaging through someone's trash or a business dumpster with the intent to obtain identity and financial information for the purpose of illegal financial gain.

Firewall: Computer protection software installed to guard against hackers and computer criminals attempting to steal passwords, credit card information and identity information.

Fraud Alert: A fraud alert is a notice placed upon a consumer's credit report in order to be notified of any suspicious activity generated by an inquiry into his/her credit.

Fraudulent: Fake or fictitious, although sometimes appearing to be authentic.

Fraudulent Accosting: To approach someone with the intention of committing a con or criminal scheme upon that person for the purpose of taking that person's money.

Herb: A derogatory name for a victim.

Identity: Identity means any piece of personal information unique to a person such as date of birth, social security number, credit card number, bank account number, etcetera.

Identity Criminal: Also referred to as an identity thief or imposter, an identity criminal is anyone who uses someone's identity information without their permission.

Identity Theft: A crime in which a person's personal information is stolen, without their permission, with the intention of using it for the identity thieves' own benefit.

Identity Theft Affidavit (ITA): A pre-written affidavit, designed by the Federal Trade Commission, that can be used by victims of identity theft for the purpose of creating a supporting deposition to establish the victim's identity, that the identity was stolen without the victim's permission, what law enforcement agency, if any, has filed an official identity theft report, and other pertinent information. The Identity Theft Affidavit is to be completed by the victim and can be distributed to credit reporting companies, law enforcement authorities, merchants, prosecutors, and other entities, public and private, related to the victim's case.

Identity Theft Protection Scam: A scam in the form of an email, letter, or telemarketing call to a prospective victim in which the perpetrator offers to sell protection insurance or information to protect against identity theft.

Internet Schemes: Any con or scheme that is perpetrated via the Internet, such as spam emails to obtain victims, fraudulent websites to steal victim's identity and financial information, or other messages or sites established or sent to steal money from victims.

IRS Scheme: The IRS Scheme is perpetrated by sending a letter to a prospective victim in an official looking fraudulent IRS envelope requesting the person to fax or return mail the fraudulent fill-in-the-blank IRS form (IRS W-9095) with the intention of obtaining the victim's identity information. This scheme is usually perpetrated during tax season and the address and/or fax number given is not an IRS location and is manned by the criminal.

IRS W-9095: The Application Form for Certificate Status/Ownership for Withholding Tax is a fraudulent form that looks like an IRS tax form asking for identity information such as name, address, date of birth, bank account numbers, PIN numbers, passwords and social security numbers.

Jurisdiction: The specific government agency having authority and legal ability to act upon a criminal act.

Mail Theft: Mail delivered by the post office is stolen, usually, from the home for the purpose of obtaining identity information, credit cards, checks or banking information.

Mark: A name given to a victim who has been marked, or targeted, for a con, fraud or identity theft.

Means of Identification: Any identity document such as a Social Security Number, Credit Card, Driver's License, Financial Information, as well as a Cellular Telephone Electronic Serial Number, calling card numbers, etc…

Mirror Site: A web page, sometimes created and used to commit a fraud that is nearly identical to the original authentic web page but will have a different URL.

Nigerian Email or letter scam: A con game that originated in Nigeria and perpetrated by Nigerian criminals in which an email or letter is sent to a prospective victim.

Online Auction Fraud: A fraud committed on popular auction sites, such as eBay and Yahoo, in which an unsuspecting victim purchases an item for a low price that is never delivered, or the seller tries to get the victim's identity information.

Opt-out: When a consumer chooses to enforce the option of not receiving junk mail or bothersome advertising.

Overhear Scheme: A scheme committed by an identity thief in which the thief listens for identity information given by the victim, verbally, to financial institutions, credit authorities, stores or any other place in which such information would be given.

Phishing: Also called *Carding,* Phishing is a high-tech scam that uses spam emails to deceive consumers into disclosing their credit card numbers, bank account information, Social Security numbers, passwords, and other sensitive information.

Power and Authority: Also known as a P & A, is a written document, or affidavit, authorizing someone to act on someone else's behalf or to do something in place of that person.

Scheme to Defraud: The legal term used to refer, or describe, a con or scam perpetrated or designed to commit a fraud on an unsuspecting victim.

Shoulder Surfing: When a criminal looks over a victim's shoulder for the purpose of obtaining a means of identification.

Skimmer: See *Swipe Tool*.

Spam: Junk email sent to the inboxes of Internet users.

Supporting Deposition: A written statement made that gives supporting information in the place of personal appearance testimony in which a person swears and affirms the statement is true. In an identity theft case, a victim will use a supporting deposition to establish that he/she was the victim of a crime and did not authorize anyone to use their identity.

Swipe Tool: A device used to secretly swipe a credit card through in order to steal the account information.

Telemarketing Scam: Phony telemarketers calling people for the purpose of stealing identity information such as credit card information, social security numbers, and other personal data.

URL: An abbreviation for **U**niform **R**esource **L**ocator which is the global address of documents and web pages on the World Wide Web.

Vic: Slang or abbreviation for a victim.

White Plastic: A term used to refer to the crime of illegally manufacturing credit cards by using stolen numbers and embossing them onto the blank plastic credit card, and transferring account information into the magnetic strip on the "fake" credit card.

Also provided by CTS Associates Incorporated:

PRODUCTS

The Pocketguide Series published by Looseleaf Law

SERVICES

Protective Services
Private Investigation

TRAINING COURSES

Basic Gang Identification Course
Gang Interdiction Course (LEO)
Street Smarts: A Crime Prevention Course
Interview and Interrogation
Hostage Negotiation Course
Dignitary and Executive Protection Course
Language Immersion Courses

….plus many more courses available

UPCOMING SEMINARS

Dealing with Gangs Effectively: The Seminar
Terrorism: *The threat in the US*

**For more information on our
products, upcoming seminars,
and services, contact:**

CTS Associates Incorporated, Post Office Box 1001
Patchogue, New York 11772-0800, **877-444-1287**

Email us at AJBCTS@cs.com
or visit our website at www.ctsassociatesinc.com

Facial Composite Software

Anyone can be a Forensic Artist with
FACES 4.0
The Ultimate Composite Software
Now sold by CTS Associates Inc.

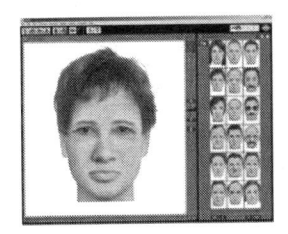

For more information and pricing
Call 877-444-1287

PROTECT YOURSELF, YOUR AGENCY AND YOUR COMMUNITY!

ID Theft Cases Are at Epidemic Levels

Do you have the knowledge needed to *prevent – investigate – prosecute* this complex crime?

Based on the personal experience of the co-authors and four subsequent years of research and applied experience with victims, tracking criminals online in the crime lab of Michigan State University (MSU) Identity Theft Partnerships in Prevention.

- Easy-to-understand
- Step-by-step training guide
- Packed with current, national recognized counter-theft expertise

BONUS! Free with purchase –
A Victims' Guide for Identity Theft

1-889031-87-9 **$21.95** + $6.00 P/H & Sales Tax
Looseleaf Law Publications, Inc. (800) 647-5547